The Complete Guide to De Vietnamese Recipes

Exploring the Secrets of Vietnamese Cooking

The Essential Vietnamese Cookbooks

By: Samantha Rich

© Copyright 2023 Samantha Rich, All Rights Reserved.

License Notes

The material presented in this book is the sole intellectual property of the author and is safeguarded by copyright laws. Without written permission from the author, it is strictly prohibited to copy, publish, or distribute any portion or all of the content.

The author has taken great care to ensure the accuracy of the information provided, making it a valuable educational resource. It is the responsibility of the reader to handle the book with care, as the author will not be held responsible for any misuse or resulting consequences.

Table of Contents

Introduction 5

Mouth-Watering Vietnamese Meals 7

   1. Healthy Prawn Salad 8

   2. Hot and Sour Fish Soup 11

   3. Vietnamese Style Caramel Trout 14

   4. Vietnamese Style Chicken Baguettes 17

   5. Tasty Seafood Salad 20

   6. Vietnamese Lamb Shanks with Sweet Potatoes 23

   7. Vietnamese Chicken Salad 26

   8. Vietnamese Style Veggie Hotpot 29

   9. Oriental Style Duck Salad 32

   10. Hearty Salmon Noodle Soup 34

   11. Basic Garlic Noodles 36

   12. Prawn Spring Roll Wraps 38

   13. Vietnamese Style Lemongrass Chicken 41

   14. Asian Style Noodle and Turkey Soup 44

15. Vietnamese Style Tau Hu Ky 47

16. Asian Style Pineapple and Prawn Salad 50

17. Classic Vietnamese Goi Cuon 52

18. Spicy Chicken Meatballs with Noodles and Broth 55

19. Savory Sea Bass with Sizzled Ginger and Onions 58

20. Classic Pok Pok Wings 60

21. Vietnamese Style Pork and Rice Noodle Salad 63

22. Vietnamese Style Caramel Chicken 65

23. Lemongrass and Sriracha Spiced Grilled Shrimp 68

24. Classic Grilled Chicken Banh Mi 71

25. Crab and Tamarind and Chili 73

Afterword's 76

Introduction

One bite of a modern Vietnamese meal seems to have the mystical power to transport diners to culinary nirvana. The reason is that Vietnamese cuisine is able to showcase not just one but five very unique flavors. Every truly good Vietnamese dish will be a medley of tastes that leave you wanting more.

You will learn how to employ a wide variety of ingredients that contribute to the distinctive flavor of many Vietnamese dishes. You'll find more than 25 of the best ingredients and recipes for Vietnamese breakfast, lunch, and dinner inside *"The Ultimate Guide to Tasty Vietnamese Recipes"*.

To that end, let's stop dithering and get to work.

HHHHHHHHHHHHHHHHHHHHHHHHHH

Mouth-Watering Vietnamese Meals

1. Healthy Prawn Salad

Serving Sizes: 2 Servings

Preparation Time: 20 Minutes

Ingredients:

For the dressing:

- 1 clove of garlic, finely chopped
- 1 small red chili, deseeded and finely chopped
- 1 tablespoon of golden caster sugar
- Juice of 2 fresh limes

For the salad:

- 1 cup of rice noodles
- 1/2 cup of fully cooked tiger prawns, cut into halves
- 1/2 cucumber, peeled, deseeded and cut into small matchsticks
- 1 carrot, cut into small matchsticks
- 6 spring onions, finely shredded
- 1 handful of fresh mint leaves, roughly chopped
- 1 tablespoon of roasted peanuts, finely chopped

HHHHHHHHHHHHHHHHHHHHHHHHHH

Methods:

a) First, make the dressing. Begin by mashing the garlic, sugar and chili together until they form a paste.
b) Add fresh lime juice and three spoonfuls of water to the mixture. Stir thoroughly to combine and set aside for later use.
c) Cook the noodles in boiling water for approximately 10 minutes or until they are tender to the touch. Once they are tender, drain the noodles and divide them between two serving bowls.
d) In a separate bowl, mix together the prawns, cucumber, carrots and onions until the ingredients are evenly mixed.
e) Serve the prawn mixture over the noodles in the serving bowls.
f) Top off the dish with coriander leaves and chopped peanuts. Serve immediately and enjoy.

2. Hot and Sour Fish Soup

Serving Sizes: 4 Servings

Preparation Time: 45 Minutes

List of Ingredients:

- 1 teaspoon of coriander seeds
- 1 small piece of ginger, thinly sliced
- 3 ½ cups of fish stock, preferably homemade
- ¾ cup of thin rice noodles
- 2 tablespoons of fish sauce
- 2 red chilies, thinly sliced and deseeded
- 3 cloves of garlic, thinly sliced
- 1 ¼ cup of raw tiger prawns, with tails on
- 7 ounces of salmon filet, cut into small cubes
- 4 spring onions, finely chopped
- 1 handful of fresh coriander leaves
- 1 handful of fresh mint leaves, roughly torn
- Juice of 2 fresh limes

HHHHHHHHHHHHHHHHHHHHHHHHHHHH

Methods:

a) Begin by placing the coriander seeds and ginger slices into a medium-sized saucepan.
b) Pour the stock into the saucepan and bring it to a boil over medium heat. Let it simmer for 5 minutes.
c) Allow the mixture to stand for 10 minutes.
d) While the broth is simmering, cook the noodles according to the instructions on the package. Once cooked, drain and set aside to keep warm.
e) Return the broth to a boil and add the fish sauce, sliced chilies, and sliced garlic. Reduce the heat to low and let it simmer for 2 minutes.
f) Add the prawns and salmon filets to the broth mixture. Let it simmer for 5 minutes or until the prawns and salmon are fully cooked through and firm to the touch.
g) Add the chopped onions, coriander, mint leaves, and fresh lime juice to the mixture.
h) Divide the cooked noodles among the serving bowls.
i) Divide the prawn and salmon mixture among the bowls, seasoning with the broth. Serve immediately and enjoy.

3. Vietnamese Style Caramel Trout

Serving Sizes: 2 Servings

Preparation Time: 20 Minutes

List of Ingredients:

- ¼ cup of golden caster sugar
- 1 tablespoon of Thai fish sauce
- 1 red chili, finely sliced
- 1 piece of ginger, finely sliced
- 2 rainbow trout filets
- 2 heads of fresh bok choy, cut in half
- ½ fresh lemon, juiced
- Fresh coriander sprigs, roughly chopped
- Steamed rice, for serving

HHHHHHHHHHHHHHHHHHHHHHHHHH

Methods:

a) Prepare the caramel sauce: Begin by placing the sugar in a large shallow pan and add a little water. Place the pan over medium heat and stir until the sugar dissolves completely.

b) Cook the caramel sauce: Increase the heat to high and allow the sugar to continue cooking until it turns an amber color.

c) Add ingredients: Add the Thai fish sauce, sliced chili, ginger, and a spoonful of water. Stir well to combine.

d) Bring to a boil: Allow the mixture to come to a boil before adding the fish filets to the pan, skin side down.

e) Add bok choy: Add the halved bok choy to the pan.

f) Simmer: Cover the pan and let the mixture simmer for about 4-5 minutes, or until the fish is cooked through and the bok choy has wilted slightly.

g) Finish the dish: Turn off the heat and squeeze fresh lemon juice over the top of the dish.

h) Garnish: Sprinkle some chopped coriander leaves over the top.

i) Serve: Serve the fish and bok choy over a bed of steamed rice and enjoy immediately.

4. Vietnamese Style Chicken Baguettes

Serving Sizes: 1 Serving

Preparation Time: 35 Minutes

List of Ingredients:

- 1 small chicken breast
- 1 tsp of extra virgin olive oil
- 1 tsp of rice vinegar
- 1/2 tsp of golden caster sugar
- Juice of 1/2 fresh lime
- 1/2 small-sized fresh carrot, peeled and grated
- 2 spring onions, thinly sliced
- 1 fresh cucumber, deseeded and thinly sliced
- 1/2 red chili, thinly sliced
- 1 baguette of your choice
- 3-4 washed gem lettuce leaves
- 1-2 tbsp of sweet chili sauce

HHHHHHHHHHHHHHHHHHHHHHHHHHH

Methods:

a) Preheat a griddle pan over high heat. While waiting, prepare the chicken breast by seasoning it with salt and pepper.

b) Place the chicken breast on the griddle pan with some olive oil. Cook for 2 to 3 minutes on each side or until fully cooked. Once done, set it aside and let it cool before shredding it into small pieces.

c) In a medium-sized bowl, combine the rice vinegar, golden caster sugar, and freshly squeezed lime juice. Stir well until the sugar dissolves.

d) Add the grated carrots, sliced spring onions, thinly sliced red chili, and cucumber into the bowl. Mix all the ingredients together.

e) Slice the baguette in half lengthwise and fill it with gem lettuce leaves.

f) Top with the shredded chicken and spoon the carrot mixture over it. Drizzle the sweet chili sauce over the top and serve immediately.

5. Tasty Seafood Salad

Serving Sizes: 5 Servings

Preparation Time: 10 Minutes

Ingredients for Your Salad:

- 5 cups of cooked seafood mix
- 25 cups of thin rice noodles, cooked
- 25 cups of freshly cooked bean sprouts
- 3 fresh carrots, thinly sliced
- 1 bunch of thinly sliced spring onions
- 1 bunch of roughly chopped fresh mint
- 1 bunch of roughly chopped fresh coriander leaves

For the dressing:

- 5 tablespoons of rice wine vinegar
- 1 teaspoon of caster sugar
- 1 finely chopped red chili
- 1 thinly sliced stick of lemongrass
- 1 tablespoon of low-sodium soy sauce

HHHHHHHHHHHHHHHHHHHHHHHHHHH

Methods:

a) Begin by preparing your salad. Take a large bowl and add your fully cooked seafood mix, rice noodles, cooked bean sprouts, sliced carrots, thinly sliced spring onions, and roughly chopped mint and coriander leaves.

b) Toss the salad ingredients roughly to combine and set the bowl aside.

c) Next, prepare your salad dressing. Take a medium-sized bowl and add the rice wine vinegar, caster sugar, finely chopped red chili, thinly sliced lemongrass, and low-sodium soy sauce.

d) Mix the ingredients well until the dressing is smooth in consistency and evenly mixed.

e) Pour the dressing over the salad and toss again to ensure that the salad is evenly coated.

f) Serve the salad immediately and enjoy your delicious meal.

6. Vietnamese Lamb Shanks with Sweet Potatoes

Serving Sizes: 4 Servings

Preparation Time: 3 Hours and 20 Minutes

List of Ingredients:

- 2 tablespoons of groundnut oil
- 4 lamb shanks
- 2 onions, halved
- 2 tablespoons of fresh ginger, finely chopped
- 3 cloves of garlic, finely sliced
- 2 red chilies, deseeded and finely chopped
- 1 tablespoon of light brown sugar-packed
- 3-star anise
- 2 stalks of lemongrass, leaves removed
- 1 ½ cups of lamb stock (preferably homemade)
- 1 ½ tablespoons of tomato puree
- 4 sweet potatoes, peeled and cut into small pieces
- 2 tablespoons of fish sauce
- 2 fresh limes, juiced
- 1 handful of fresh mint leaves, torn
- 1 handful of fresh basil leaves, torn

HHHHHHHHHHHHHHHHHHHHHHHHHHHH

Methods:

a) Preheat your oven to a temperature of 320°F.
b) Heat a spoonful of oil in a large skillet over medium-high heat.
c) Once the oil is hot enough, add in your lamb shanks and brown them for at least 2 minutes on all sides.
d) Remove the lamb shanks from the skillet and set them aside.
e) In the same skillet, add more oil and fry the onion for about 30 seconds.
f) Add the ginger, garlic, and chili and continue cooking for an additional minute on low heat.
g) Add the sugar, star anise, stalks of lemongrass, lamb stock, tomato puree, mint leaves, and basil leaves to the skillet. Stir well to combine all the ingredients.
h) Cover the skillet and place it in the preheated oven. Let it cook for about 1 ½ hours.
i) Add the sweet potatoes to the skillet and cook for another hour or until the lamb is completely cooked through.
j) Once the lamb and sweet potatoes are cooked, add fish sauce, fresh lemon juice, and the remaining teaspoon of sugar. Stir well to combine and serve hot.

7. Vietnamese Chicken Salad

Serving Sizes: 3 Servings

Preparation Time: 20 Minutes

List of Ingredients:

- ½ Cup of Rice Noodles, Thai Variety
- 1 Carrot, Fresh, Peeled, and Finely Diced
- ½ of a Cucumber, Fresh
- 2 Chicken Breasts, Fully Cooked and Finely Shredded
- ¼ Cup of Radishes, Sliced Thinly
- ½ of a Red Onion, Thinly Sliced
- 1 Bunch of Mint, Small in Size, and Leaves Picked
- 3 tablespoons of Peanuts, Roasted and Chopped Roughly

Ingredients for Your Dressing:

- 1 Red Chili, Small in Size, Deseeded, and Finely Chopped
- 1 Lime, Juice, and Zest Only
- 1 ½ tablespoons of Fish Sauce
- 1 ½ tablespoons of Soy Sauce, Your Favorite Kind
- 1 ½ tablespoons of Oil, Sesame Variety

HHHHHHHHHHHHHHHHHHHHHHHHHH

Methods:

a) Begin by making your dressing. In a medium-sized bowl, add all the ingredients for your dressing and whisk until thoroughly combined.

b) Cook your rice noodles according to the directions on the package. Once cooked, drain and add them to the bowl with your dressing. Toss them to combine with the dressing.

c) Peel your carrot and cucumber, then slice them into long thin strips. Add them to the bowl with your noodle mixture.

d) Finely shred the fully cooked chicken breasts and add them to the bowl with the other ingredients.

e) Slice the radishes thinly and add them to the bowl with the other ingredients.

f) Add thinly sliced red onion and small mint leaves to the bowl with the other ingredients. Toss everything together to combine. Serve with a garnish of roughly chopped roasted peanuts.

8. Vietnamese Style Veggie Hotpot

Serving Sizes: 4 Servings

Preparation Time: 25 Minutes

List of Ingredients:

- 2 teaspoons of Oil, Vegetable Variety
- 1 Piece of Ginger Root, Fresh and Finely Shredded
- 2 Cloves of Garlic, Finely Chopped
- ½ of a Butternut Squash, Large in Size, Peeled and Cut into Small Sized Pieces
- 2 teaspoons of Soy Sauce, Your Favorite Kind
- 2 teaspoons of Brown Sugar, Light and Packed
- ¾ Cup of Vegetable Stock, Homemade Preferable
- ½ Cup of Green Beans, Fresh, Trimmed and Thinly Sliced
- 4 Onions, Spring Variety and Thinly Sliced
- A Dash of Coriander Leaves, Fresh and for Garnish
- Some Basmati Rice, For Serving and Fully Cooked

HHHHHHHHHHHHHHHHHHHHHHHHHH

Methods:

a) Begin by heating up your oil in a medium-sized saucepan over medium heat.
b) Once the oil is hot, add in your finely chopped ginger and garlic, stirring well to combine. Cook for at least 5 minutes, stirring frequently to prevent burning.
c) Next, add in your diced squash, your favorite kind of soy sauce, and vegetable stock. Stir thoroughly to combine.
d) Cover the saucepan and allow the mixture to simmer for the next 10 minutes, stirring occasionally to ensure even cooking.
e) Remove the lid and add in your trimmed green beans. Continue to cook for another 3 minutes or until the green beans are tender.
f) Add in your sliced onions and continue cooking for an additional minute until the onions are softened.
g) Remove the saucepan from the heat.
h) Serve your squash and green bean stir-fry over a bed of rice and sprinkle with fresh coriander leaves as a garnish

9. Oriental Style Duck Salad

Serving Sizes: 2 Servings

Preparation Time: 40 Minutes

List of Ingredients:

- 1 Duck Leg
- 1 teaspoon of Five Spice, Chinese Variety and Powdered
- ½ Cup of Noodles, Rice Variety
- 1 Stick of Celery, Cut into Small Sized Matchsticks
- 1 Carrot, Fresh, and Cut into Small Sized Matchstick
- ½ of a Cucumber, Fresh, Deseeded, and Cut into Small Sized Matchsticks
- 2 Onions, Spring Variety and Thinly Sliced
- 2 tablespoons of Hoisin Sauce
- 1 tablespoon of Soy Sauce, Your Favorite Kind

HHHHHHHHHHHHHHHHHHHHHHHHHHH

Methods:

a) Preheat your oven to a temperature of 430°F.
b) Rub the Chinese-style five-spice powder all over your duck leg.
c) Place the duck leg onto a large baking tray and roast in the preheated oven.
d) Cook the rice noodles according to the directions on the package, drain, and set aside.
e) Chop celery, carrot, cucumber, and onions and add to a large bowl. Add in the cooked noodles and toss to combine.
f) Once the duck leg is cooked, remove the meat from the bone and shred it finely using two forks.
g) Make the dressing by whisking together hoisin sauce, your favorite soy sauce, and two spoonfuls of water in a small bowl. Drizzle the dressing over the salad, top with shredded duck meat, and serve immediately.

10. Hearty Salmon Noodle Soup

Serving Sizes: 4 Servings

Preparation Time: 35 Minutes

List of Ingredients:

- 2 Cups of Chicken Stock, Low in Sodium and Homemade Preferable
- 2 teaspoons of Curry Pasta, Red Thai Variety
- ½ Cup of Noodles, Rice Variety, and Flat
- ½ Cup of Mushrooms, Shiitake Variety, and Thinly Sliced
- ½ Cup of Corn, Baby Variety, and Thinly Sliced
- 2 Salmon Fillets, Skinless Variety and Thinly Sliced
- 2 Limes, Fresh and Juice Only
- 1 tablespoon of Soy Sauce, Low in Salt and Your Favorite Kind
- A Dash of Brown Sugar, Light, and Packed
- 1 Bunch of Coriander, Fresh and Roughly Chopped

HHHHHHHHHHHHHHHHHHHHHHHHHHH

Methods:

a) Start by pouring your stock into a large-sized pan and bringing it to a boil.
b) Once your mixture is boiling, add your curry paste and noodles. Allow your noodles to cook for at least 8 minutes or until they are tender.
c) After this time, add in your mushrooms and corn. Continue to cook for another 2 minutes.
d) Add your salmon and continue to cook for another 3 minutes or until your salmon is fully cooked through.
e) Remove the dish from the heat and add in your fresh lime juice, your favorite kind of soy sauce, and a dash of brown sugar.
f) Stir the mixture thoroughly to combine.
g) Serve the dish with a garnish of coriander for added flavor.
h) Enjoy your delicious salmon curry noodle soup!

11. Basic Garlic Noodles

Serving Sizes: 3 to 4 Servings

Preparation Time: 20 Minutes

List of Ingredients:

- 20 Ounces of Noodles, Yellow in Color
- 1 tablespoon of Parmesan Cheese, Freshly Grated
- Some Water, For Boiling
- Ingredients for Your Garlic Sauce:
- 1 Stick of Butter, Unsalted Variety
- 2 tablespoons of Garlic, Minced
- 1 tablespoon of Maggi Seasoning
- 1 tablespoon of Oyster Sauce
- 1 tablespoon of Fish Sauce
- 1 tablespoon of Sugar, White in Color

HHHHHHHHHHHHHHHHHHHHHHHHHHHH

Methods:

a) Rinse the noodles under running water and then drain them. Set them aside for later use.
b) Heat a pot of water to a boil. Add the noodles and cook them until they are soft. Drain them and set them aside to dry.
c) In a large pan set over low to medium heat, melt the butter. Once melted, add the garlic and cook until it turns brown and aromatic.
d) Add the Maggie seasoning, oyster sauce, fish sauce, and sugar to the pan. Stir to combine the ingredients. Remove from heat.
e) Add the cooked noodles to the pan and toss them thoroughly to coat them with the sauce.
f) Top the noodles with cheese.
g) Serve immediately.

12. Prawn Spring Roll Wraps

Serving Sizes: 4 Servings

Preparation Time: 30 Minutes

List of Ingredients:

- ¼ Cup of Noodles, Rice Variety, and Dried
- 1 tablespoon of Oil, Sunflower Variety
- 1 ¼ Cup of Vegetables, Stir Fry Variety
- ½ of a Ginger Root, Fresh and Finely Grated
- 1 Bunch of Coriander, Small in Size, Stalks Finely Sliced and Chopped Roughly
- ¾ Cup of Prawns, Raw, Peeled and Cut into Halves
- 2 tablespoons of Chili Sauce, Sweet Variety and for Serving
- 8 Sheets of Filo Pastry, Small in Size
- 1 tablespoon of Sesame Seeds, Optional and Lightly Toasted

HHHHHHHHHHHHHHHHHHHHHHHHHH

Methods:

a) Preheat the oven to a temperature of 430°F.
b) Cook the noodles according to the instructions on the package.
c) Heat oil in a large wok over medium heat.
d) Add vegetables, ginger root, and coriander stalks. Stir-fry for 3-4 minutes or until almost fully cooked.
e) Add prawns and stir-fry for an additional minute or until pink in color.
f) Stir in chili sauce, fresh coriander leaves, and cooked noodles. Toss to combine and remove from heat.
g) Brush four filo sheets with oil and cover them with the remaining filo sheets.
h) Place at least ¼ cup of the prawn mixture along the narrow edge of the filo sheet. Fold and roll to form spring rolls. Repeat until all the prawn mixture is used.
i) Brush rolls with oil and sprinkle with sesame seeds.
j) Place the rolls on a greased baking sheet and bake in the oven for 15 minutes or until golden and crispy.
k) Allow them to cool slightly before serving.

13. Vietnamese Style Lemongrass Chicken

Serving Sizes: 3 Servings

Preparation Time: 12 Minutes

List of Ingredients:

- 2 tablespoons of Fish Sauce
- 3 Cloves of Garlic, Crushed
- 1 tablespoon of Curry, Powdered Variety
- ½ teaspoons of Salt, For Taste
- 2 tablespoons + ½ teaspoons of Sugar, White
- 1 ½ Pounds of Chicken Breast, Boneless, Skinless, and Cut into Small Sized Pieces
- 3 tablespoons of Water, Warm
- 3 tablespoons of Oil, Cooking Variety
- 2 Stalks of Lemongrass, Fresh and Minced
- 1 Shallot, Large in Size and Sliced Thinly
- 3 Chilies, Seeded and Minced
- 1 Scallion, For Garnish

HHHHHHHHHHHHHHHHHHHHHHHHHHH

Methods:

a) Use a large-sized bowl and add in your fish sauce, powdered curry, minced garlic, a dash of salt and sugar. Stir thoroughly to combine before adding in your chicken. Toss to coat.

b) Then use a small sized skillet and add in your remaining sugar with at least a spoonful of water. Cook over high heat until your sugar fully dissolves. Continue to cook until your mixture turns caramel in color.

c) Remove from heat and add in two more spoonfuls of water. Transfer this mixture to a small sized bowl.

d) Next heat up a large sized wok over high heat. Add in your oil and once it is hot enough add in your lemongrass, shallots and chilies. Stir fry until fragrant.

e) Then add in your chicken and caramel. Continue to cook until your sauce is thick in consistency. Remove from heat.

f) Serve over a bed of steamed rice and top off with your scallions. Enjoy.

14. Asian Style Noodle and Turkey Soup

Serving Sizes: 4 Servings

Preparation Time: 20 Minutes

List of Ingredients:

- 2 Cups of Chicken Stock, Homemade Preferable
- 1 Piece of Ginger Root, Peeled and Thinly Sliced
- 2 Star Anise
- 1 Stick of Cinnamon
- 3 Cloves, Whole
- ¾ Cup of Noodles, Rice Variety and Dried
- 2 to 3 tablespoons of Fish Sauce
- 2 Limes, Fresh and Juice Only
- 1 ½ Cups of Turkey, Fully Cooked, Roasted and Finely Shredded
- ½ Cup of Bean Sprouts, Bagged Variety
- A Dash of Coriander, Fresh and Chopped Roughly
- A Dash of Mint, Fresh and Roughly Chopped
- 4 Onions, Spring Variety and Thinly Sliced
- 2 Chilies, Red in Color and Thinly Sliced

HHHHHHHHHHHHHHHHHHHHHHHHHHH

Methods:

a) Pour your stock into a large-sized pan. Add in your sliced ginger, star anise, and a stick of cinnamon and cloves. Set to a simmer over medium heat and allow to simmer for the next 10 minutes.

b) Next, soak your noodles according to the directions on the package. Once soaked, drain and rinse your noodles.

c) Add your fish sauce and fresh lime juice to your chicken stock.

d) Divide your ready noodles into four even-sized bowls and top off with your shredded turkey, beansprouts, coriander leaves, mint leaves, red chilies, and onions. Stir thoroughly to combine.

e) Ladle your stock over your noodles and squeeze some lime juice over the top. Serve and enjoy.

15. Vietnamese Style Tau Hu Ky

Serving Sizes: 4 Servings

Preparation Time: 20 Minutes

List of Ingredients:

- 1 Pound of Shrimp, Raw
- 4 Pieces of Bean Curd Skin, Dry
- 1 Clove of Garlic, Minced
- 3 Pieces of Ginger, Fresh and Sliced Thinly
- 1/8 teaspoon of Salt, For Taste
- ¼ teaspoon of Sugar, White in Color
- 1 Egg, White Only and Beaten Thoroughly
- 1 Stalk of Scallion, Finely Chopped
- A Dash of White Pepper, Powdered Variety
- 2 teaspoons of Oil, Vegetable or Peanut Variety

HHHHHHHHHHHHHHHHHHHHHHHHHHH

Methods:

a) The first thing that you will want to do is rinse and devein a shrimp. Once you have done this, dry your shrimp with a few paper towels.

b) Then add your shrimp, minced garlic, ginger, a dash of white pepper and oil of your choice into a food processor. Blend on the highest setting until a paste begins to form. Transfer your paste to a large-sized bowl.

c) Add your shrimp to this bowl and toss thoroughly to coat.

d) Add in your beaten egg white and chopped scallions and toss again to combine.

e) Place your bean curd skin onto a flat surface and wipe the surface of the skin with a damp towel until soft to the touch.

f) Place a spoonful of your shrimp paste into the center of your skin and roll burrito style. Repeat until all of your fillings have been used.

g) Heat up a large-sized wok with some oil for your choice over high heat. Once the oil is hot enough add in your rolls and fry until golden brown in color. This should take at least 5 to 10 minutes.

h) Serve your rolls with your chili garlic sauce. Enjoy.

16. Asian Style Pineapple and Prawn Salad

Serving Sizes: 4 Servings

Preparation Time: 20 Minutes

List of Ingredients:

- 1 Pineapple, Small in Size and Cut into Small Sized Chunks
- ½ Cup of Bean Sprouts, Fresh
- 1 Cup of Prawns, King Variety and Fully Cooked
- ½ of a Cucumber, Peeled, Deseeded and Sliced Thinly
- ¾ Cup of Tomatoes, Cherry Variety and Sliced into Halves
- 1 Handful of Mint Leaves, Fresh and Chopped Roughly
- ¼ Cup of Cashews, Unsalted Variety and Lightly Toasted
- Ingredients for Your Dressing:
- ½ of a Red Chili, Deseeded and Thinly Sliced
- 1 Clove of Garlic, Minced
- 1 teaspoon of Sugar, Golden Caster Variety
- 2 Limes, Juice Only and Fresh
- 1 ½ teaspoons of Fish Sauce

HHHHHHHHHHHHHHHHHHHHHHHHHH

Methods:

a) First mash your chili, minced garlic, and caster sugar into a paste until smooth in consistency.

b) Add in your fresh lime juice and fish sauce. Stir again until evenly mixed and set aside for later use.

c) Next, toss your beansprouts, king prawns, fresh cucumber, tomato and two spoonfuls of your dressing. Toss thoroughly until completely mixed.

d) Serve with a garnish of your mint leaves and cashews. Drizzle your remaining dressing over the top and serve right away.

17. Classic Vietnamese Goi Cuon

Serving Sizes: 4 Servings

Preparation Time: 15 Minutes

Ingredients for Your Grilled Pork:

- 1 Pound of Pork Chops, Sliced thinly
- 2 Cloves of Garlic, Minced
- 2 Shallots, Minced
- 1 tablespoon of Fish Sauce
- 1 teaspoon of Sugar, White in Color
- 2 teaspoons of Black Pepper, For Taste
- ¼ Cup of Oil, Vegetable or Peanut Variety

Ingredients for Your Hoisin Peanut Dipping Sauce:

- 1 Cup of Hoisin Sauce
- ¼ Cup of Peanut Butter, Smooth Variety
- 1 tablespoon of Vinegar, Rice Variety
- 2 Cloves of Garlic, Crushed
- 1 Thai Style Chili, Minced

Ingredients for Your Spring Rolls:

- 10 Rice Paper Wrappers
- Some Lettuce, Fresh
- Some Cucumber, Fresh, and Cut into Slices
- Some Fresh Mint, For Garnish
- Some Basil, For Garnish
- Some Coriander, Vietnamese Style, and for Garnish

HHHHHHHHHHHHHHHHHHHHHHHHHHH

Methods:

a) Use a large sized plastic bag and add in all of your ingredients for your pork into it. Toss thoroughly to combine and allow to marinate for the next 20 minutes.

b) After this time, grill your pork on all sides for the next 2 to 3 minutes or until done to your liking.

c) Then use a blender and add in all of your ingredients for your peanut sauce. Blend on the highest setting until smooth in consistency.

d) Next use a large sized bowl and add in some water. Dip each of your rice papers into it for no more than 5 seconds.

e) Layer some lettuce, cucumber, basil, mint and coriander onto your rolls. Top off with your pork and roll burrito style.

f) Serve with your freshly made hoisin sauce and enjoy.

18. Spicy Chicken Meatballs with Noodles and Broth

Serving Sizes: 6 Servings

Preparation Time: 1 Hour and 20 Minutes

List of Ingredients:

- 1 Onion, Large in Size and Chopped Roughly
- 1 Piece of Ginger Root, Fresh
- 1 to 2 Red Chilies, Finely Chopped
- 1 Clove of Garlic, Crushed
- 6 Peppercorns, White in Color and Crushed Finely
- ¼ Cup of Coriander Leaves, Fresh and Chopped Roughly
- ¼ Cup of Milk, Whole
- ½ Cup of Breadcrumbs, Fresh and White in Color
- 2 ¼ Pounds of Chicken Mince
- 3 tablespoons of Oil, Vegetable Variety

Ingredients for Your Broth:

- 2 Cups of Chicken Stock, Homemade Preferable
- 2 tablespoons of Sesame Oil, Lightly Toasted
- 3 tablespoons of Fish Sauce
- 6 Star Anise
- 1 Piece of Ginger Root, Fresh and Thinly Sliced
- ½ teaspoons of Peppercorns, Black in Color
- 8 Onions, Spring Variety and Thinly Sliced
- 1 ¼ Cup of Noodles, Egg Variety and Thinly Sliced
- Some Chilies, Thinly Sliced and for Taste
- 1 Bunch of Basil, Small in Size, Leaves Picked and Roughly Chopped

HHHHHHHHHHHHHHHHHHHHHHHHH

Methods:

a) Place your onions, ginger, chilies, garlic, white peppercorns and half of your coriander stalks into a food processor. Pulse until finely chopped.

b) Add in your milk and breadcrumbs into a large sized bowl. Then add in your pulsed onion mix and your chicken mince into your breadcrumb mixture and mix thoroughly until combined.

c) Shape your breadcrumb mixture into even small sized balls.

d) Next place a large sized pan over medium heat and add in a touch of oil. Once your oil is hot enough add in your meatballs and cook for the next 10 minutes until thoroughly brown in color.

e) Next, make your broth. To do this add your stock into a large sized saucepan and bring to a boil. Once boiling reduce the heat and bring to a simmer.

f) Then add in your oil, fish sauce, ginger, coriander stalks, star anise and black peppercorns. Allow it to simmer for the next 20 minutes.

g) After this time add in your onions, noodles and red chilies if you are using them.

h) Serve your broth with your meatballs served over the top and season with your basil.

19. Savory Sea Bass with Sizzled Ginger and Onions

Serving Sizes: 6 Servings

Preparation Time: 25 Minutes

List of Ingredients:

- 6 Sea Bass Filets, Skin On and Scaled
- 3 tablespoons of Oil, Sunflower Variety
- 1 Piece of Ginger, Peeled and Shredded
- 3 Cloves of Garlic, Sliced Thinly
- 3 Red Chilies, Deseeded Variety and thinly Shredded
- 1 Bunch of Spring Onions, Finely Shredded
- 1 tablespoon of Soy Sauce, Your Favorite Kind

HHHHHHHHHHHHHHHHHHHHHHHHHHHH

Methods:

a) The first thing that you will want to do is season your fish with a dash of salt and pepper. Slash the skin at least three times.

b) Then heat up some oil in a large sized pan. Once your oil is hot enough add in your fish with the skin side down. Cook for the next 5 minutes or until the skin is crispy and golden in color. Flip and continue to cook for an additional minute. After this time remove and place onto a serving plate. Set aside for later use.

c) Next heat up your remaining oil in your saucepan again. Once your oil is hot enough add in your ginger, garlic and red chilies. Cook for at least two minutes or until golden in color.

d) Remove from heat and add in your spring onions.

e) Add a drizzle of soy sauce and add your cooked onion mixture over the top. Serve while still piping hot and enjoy.

20. Classic Pok Pok Wings

Serving Sizes: 3 to 4 Servings

Preparation Time: 30 Minutes

List of Ingredients:

- ¼ Cup of Fish Sauce
- ¼ Cup of Sugar, Superfine Variety
- 8 Cloves of Garlic, Crushed and Minced
- 1 ½ Pounds of Chicken Wings
- 2 tablespoons of Oil, Vegetable Variety, and for Frying
- 1/3 Cup of Cornstarch
- 1 tablespoon of Cilantro, Fresh and Roughly Chopped
- 1 tablespoon of Mint, Fresh and Roughly Chopped

HHHHHHHHHHHHHHHHHHHHHHHHHH

Methods:

a) Use a small-sized bowl and add in your fish sauce, sugar, and crushed garlic. Whisk thoroughly to combine.

b) Add your wings into this bowl and toss to coat. Cover and place into your fridge to chill for the next 3 hours, making sure to toss them occasionally.

c) After this time, heat up some oil in a small-sized skillet. Once your oil is hot enough add in your minced garlic. Cook for the next 3 minutes or until golden in color. Remove and drain on a plate lined with paper towels.

d) Then use a large sized pot and heat up at least two inches of oil. While your oil is heating up, pat your wings with paper towels.

e) Add your cornstarch into a small sized bowl and add in your wings. Toss to coat.

f) Add your coated wings to your cornstarch and fry for the next 10 minutes or until golden in color. After this time drain and transfer to a large sized bowl.

g) Then use a small sized saucepan and add in your marinade. Allow it to simmer for the next 5 minutes or until syrupy in consistency. Add in your wings and toss to coat.

h) Serve with a topping of cilantro, fresh mint and fried minced garlic.

21. Vietnamese Style Pork and Rice Noodle Salad

Serving Sizes: 4 Servings

Preparation Time: 20 Minutes

List of Ingredients:

- 1 teaspoon of Lemongrass Paste
- 1 teaspoon of Ginger Root, Freshly Grated
- ½ of a Red Chili, Chopped Finely
- 1 teaspoon of Oil, Sunflower Variety
- 3 tablespoons of Fish Sauce
- 4 Pork Chops

Ingredients for Your Salad:

- ¾ Cup of Noodles, Rice, and a Thin Variety
- 1 Lime, Fresh and Juice Only
- ½ teaspoon of Sugar, Caster Variety
- ½ of a Cucumber, Fresh and Thinly Sliced
- 1 Handful of Mint Leaves, Roughly Chopped and Fresh

HHHHHHHHHHHHHHHHHHHHHHHHHHHH

Methods:

a) First mix together your lemon paste with your ginger, chili, sunflower oil and fish sauce in a large-sized bowl until evenly mixed.
b) Spread this paste over your pork chops and set aside to marinate.
c) Next place your rice noodles into a large sized bowl. Cover your noodles with some boiling water and allow them to sit for the next 5 minutes or until they are soft to the touch. After this time, drain your noodles and place them back into your bowl.
d) Whisk your remaining fish sauce, fresh lime juice, fresh lime zest and sugar until evenly mixed. Pour this mixture over your noodles.
e) Then slice your cucumber into strips. Add to your noodles along with your mint leaves and toss thoroughly to combine.
f) Next heat up a large-sized griddle pan until piping hot. Once hot enough add in your pork chops and cook for at least 5 minutes on each side.
g) Serve with your salad and enjoy right away.

22. Vietnamese Style Caramel Chicken

Serving Sizes: 3 Servings

Preparation Time: 20 Minutes

List of Ingredients:

- 1 Pound of Chicken Thighs, With The Skin and Deboned
- 2 tablespoons of Olive Oil, Extra Virgin Variety
- 3 Cloves of Garlic, Minced
- ½ of a Jalapeno, Thinly Sliced

Ingredients for Your Marinade:

- 1 tablespoon of Sugar, White in Color
- 1 tablespoon of Fish Sauce
- A Dash of Black Pepper, For Taste

Ingredients for Your Caramel Sauce:

- 1 tablespoon of Fish Sauce
- 3 tablespoons of Water, Warm
- ½ tablespoon of Sugar, White in Color
- 3 teaspoons of Vinegar, Rice Variety

HHHHHHHHHHHHHHHHHHHHHHHHH

Methods:

a) The first thing that you will want to do is marinate your chicken. To do this add your chicken along with your remaining ingredients for your marinade into a large-sized bowl. Stir thoroughly to combine and cover with some plastic wrap. Place into your fridge to marinate for the next 10 minutes.

b) While your chicken is marinating make your caramel sauce. To do this add your ingredients for your fish sauce into a medium sized bowl. Stir thoroughly to combine.

c) Then heat up a large sized skillet placed over medium to high heat. Add in your oil and once your oil is hot enough add in your chicken. Cook for the next 5 to 10 minutes or until slightly crispy and brown in color. Transfer to a plate once cooked.

d) Add in your remaining oil to your skillet. Once your oil is hot enough add in your garlic. Cook for at least one minute.

e) Then add your chicken back to your pan along with your premade caramel sauce. Stir thoroughly to combine.

f) Reduce the heat to low and simmer for the next 5 minutes or until your sauce is thick in consistency.

g) Add in your jalapenos and continue to cook for an additional minute. Remove from heat and serve.

23. Lemongrass and Sriracha Spiced Grilled Shrimp

Serving Sizes: 6 Servings

Preparation Time: 30 Minutes

List of Ingredients:

- 1 Pound of Shrimp, Jumbo Variety, Peeled, Deveined and Tails On
- Some Oil, For Brushing

Ingredients for Your Marinade:

- 2 tablespoons of Fish Sauce
- 1 Lemongrass, White Part Only and Freshly Grated
- 1 tablespoon of Sugar, Powdered Variety
- 1 teaspoon of Sriracha
- 1 Clove of Garlic, Minced

Ingredients for Your Chili-Calamansi Dipping Sauce:

- 1 ½ tablespoons of Chili Garlic Sauce
- 1 tablespoon of Water, Warm
- ½ tablespoon of Cilantro Leaves, Fresh and Roughly Chopped
- 1 Calamansi, Small in Size and Juice Extracted

HHHHHHHHHHHHHHHHHHHHHHHHHH

Methods:

a) First clean your shrimp under some cold running water. Once rinsed pat dry with a few paper towels. Transfer into a large sized bowl.
b) Add in all of your marinade ingredients into your bowl and stir thoroughly to combine. Cover with some plastic wrap and allow to marinate for the next 15 minutes.
c) After this time, thread your shrimp onto your skewers.
d) Brush with some oil and place onto a preheated grill. Grill for at least 5 to 10 minutes or until slightly charred and fully cooked through.
e) Remove and serve immediately with your dipping sauce.

24. Classic Grilled Chicken Banh Mi

Serving Sizes: 6 Servings

Preparation Time: 1 Hour

List of Ingredients:

- 1 ½ Pounds of Chicken Thighs, Boneless, and Skinless Variety
- ¼ teaspoons of Sugar, White in Color
- ¼ teaspoons of Salt, For Taste
- 1 ¼ teaspoons of Black Pepper, For Taste
- 1 tablespoon of Fish Sauce
- 1 tablespoon of Lime Juice, Fresh
- 1 ½ tablespoons of Oil, Canola Variety

HHHHHHHHHHHHHHHHHHHHHHHHHHHH

Methods:

a) The first thing that you will want to do is trim the fat from your chicken thighs.
b) Then use a large-sized bowl and mix together your white sugar, a dash of salt, a dash of pepper, fish sauce and fresh lime juice.
c) Add in your oil and stir thoroughly to combine.
d) Next add in your chicken thighs and toss to combine. Cover with some plastic wrap and place into your fridge to marinate for the next 30 minutes.
e) After this time, grill your chicken. To do this preheat a gas grill to medium to high heat. Once it is hot enough add in your chicken and grill for the next 6 to 10 minutes, making sure to turn a couple of times until your chicken is fully cooked through.
f) Remove and allow to cool for the next 10 minutes before serving. Enjoy.

25. Crab and Tamarind and Chili

Serving Sizes: 4 Servings

Preparation Time: 35 Minutes

List of Ingredients:

- 4 Pounds of Crabs, Fresh and Scrubbed
- Some Oil, Vegetable Variety and for Frying
- 1 Egg, Large in Size
- 1 tablespoon of Tamarind, Only Juice
- 2 tablespoons of Oysters Sauce
- 1 tablespoon of Oil, Sesame Variety
- 2 tablespoons of Sugar, White in Color
- 1 Clove of Garlic, Chopped Finely
- 1 Onion, Small in Size and Cut into Thin Wedges
- 1 Red Chili, Small in Size, Fresh and Chopped Finely
- ¼ Cup of Saw Tooth Herb, Finely Chopped
- ¼ Cup of Rice Paddy Herb, Finely Chopped
- Some Steamed Rice, For Serving

HHHHHHHHHHHHHHHHHHHHHHHHHH

Methods:

a) First prepare your crab and break it apart.
b) Then heat up some oil in a large sized wok placed over high heat. Once your oil is hot enough add in your crab pieces and fry for the next 2 to 3 minutes. After this time remove and drain on a plate lined with paper towels.
c) Mix together your egg, fresh tamarind juice, oyster sauce, sesame oil and white sugar. Stir thoroughly to combine and set aside for later use.
d) Heat up some oil in a clean large sized wok set over high heat. Once your oil is hot enough add in your garlic and cook for at least 15 to 20 seconds.
e) Then add in your onions and chili. Continue to cook for another 1 to 2 minutes or until translucent.
f) Next add in your tamarind and egg mixture to your wok. Bring this mixture to a boil and allow to simmer until slightly reduced.
g) Add in your fried egg pieces, sawtooth herb and rice paddy herb. Toss thoroughly to coat. Remove from heat.
h) Serve your dish over a bed of steamed rice. Enjoy.

Afterword's

Thank you so much

Wow, what an incredible experience this has been. I couldn't have done it without your support and participation. As an author, I can only write the words, but it's up to the reader to bring them to life. And you did exactly that. You purchased this book, dedicated your time to reading it, and reached the end with me. I am deeply humbled.

While you've already done so much, I have one more request. I value feedback from my readers and would love to hear your thoughts on the book. I would be grateful if you could leave a review on Amazon. Not only will I see it, but it will also give others the opportunity to discover the book as well. The book community is a special one, and by sharing your thoughts, you are contributing to its growth and success.

Thank you for being so awesome.

Samantha Rich